Verses Of The Healing Soul

Arnab Bhowmick

BookLeaf
Publishing

India | USA | UK

Dedication

To the younger me, who bravely gambled his
heart, and to all the young boys and men who
dare to do the same—

May you find courage in your vulnerability and
strength in your pursuit of love.

In your journey, you will struggle, feel pain, and
rise from the flames,

Never giving up in the face of heartache, but
learning and growing through each challenge.

Remember, life is preparing and moulding you
for something better;

The trials you endure are but steps towards a
horizon of hope and renewal.

Acknowledgement

First and foremost, I extend my deepest gratitude to God, whose boundless grace and guidance have illuminated my path and made this journey possible. Your Divine wisdom has been my strength and inspiration.

To my parents, thank you for your unwavering support and boundless love. Your encouragement and sacrifices have shaped me into who I am today. I am forever grateful for your belief in me.

To my dear sister, your constant presence and encouragement have been a source of joy and motivation. Your understanding and support have been invaluable to me.

To my beloved wife, whose love and companionship have been my greatest treasure—thank you for your patience, understanding, and for standing by my side through every challenge. Your belief in me has been a guiding light.

Finally, my heartfelt thanks to the publisher, whose belief in this work and professional expertise have made this publication a reality. Your dedication and support have been truly remarkable.
With gratitude and love,

Arnab Bhowmick

Preface

We are all explorers in life. In the adventurous journey of life, this collection of poems weaves together threads of love, pain, and heartbreak with the wisdom of growing up anew. Each verse captures the delicate dance between the joy of love and the ache of loss, exploring the profound impact of relationships on our hearts and souls.

Love is not just an emotion, love is a journey just like life. We step into it, we understand it and we try to feel it as much as possible. We cannot win love, it will come to us in its own intriguing way and life is all about experiencing this love. We need to accept love in all its forms, the harsh and the gentle.

As we go through the seasons of our lives, we encounter moments of intense passion and deep sorrow, each shaping our understanding of ourselves and our place in the world.

 In this collection, nature is a silent spectator while playing an important role in our struggles and triumphs. The rhythms of the natural world—the various seasons, its cycles of renewal and decay, its tranquil beauty and fierce storms—echo our own experiences of love and loss. Through nature's eyes, we see reflections of our inner landscapes, offering solace and perspective as we navigate our personal love stories.

As you turn these pages, may you find resonance in the verses and solace in the shared human experience. These poems are a witness to the enduring spirit of growth and the eternal quest for meaning amidst the ever-changing tides of life.

Sweet Reminiscence of Pain

When the days are long and dull I long for
some eccentric ecstasy,
I want to be lost in the pleasant pain of old
memories.
Or dream in my own world of benevolent
butterflies,
I can imagine the advent of my beloved's
footsteps,
My ears ring with surreal symphonies.

This monotonous life with sophisticated
simplicity,
Is gnarling a part of us every day bit by bit.
The pleasant hug from you is the only elixir
that I am alive for,
What else is life other than delicate ruggedness?
We keep getting lost in the loud silence,
The more we have, the more insatiable the urge
grows.

Let's forget the world and hug each other.
Your jaw-dropping aura soothes me to sleep.
You remain only in this dream so I won't wake
up,
I will hold tight to this sweet reminiscence of
pain.

Drifting Souls

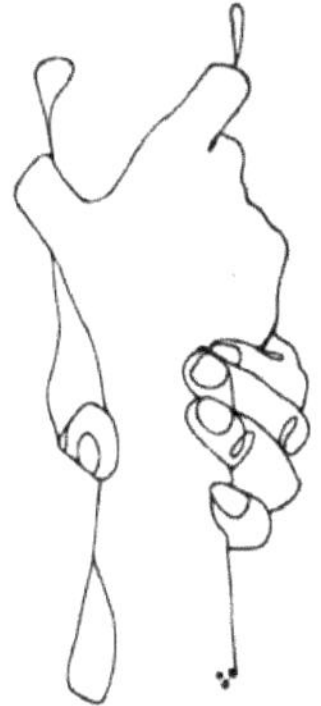

When I am at the rock bottom of my life, will
you still choose me?
When the cold breeze of the night hits my face,
And my eyes are shadowed with tears,
Your pretty face shimmers before my eyes.
I imagine the times we spent together happily,
And some intriguing questions bother me,
Was it my hug which was not tight enough?
Or was my touch not warm enough?
Was I not a good listener, was I not patient?
I still search for the reason that could not keep
you mine forever.

Let our souls drift in the skies only to touch
one last time,
Souls are innocent; they won't judge each other
for not being together,
They won't judge that the promises were not
kept,
They don't mind that "forever" may not be
eternal.
My soul is still out there searching for you,
Just believe for conversation's sake that we
meet again,
Your nonchalant smile takes my breath away,
I want this story to go on forever,
But then it's morning again and you are gone.

Do you ponder on the dreams you made me
see?
Do you think about the promises that you
made?
Or are you engaged making fresh promises to
someone new?

Let us leave this reality and meet where souls
meet,
Where there are no expectations in love.
Where I might understand the kind of love you
wanted,
So, let our souls drift in space and touch each
other.
You will finally understand the love I hold for
you,
Over there, only music exists, along with the
love of our souls.

Let's Have A Secret Dream

Dust accumulates in the dim, deserted room,
Everything veiled by a thick, muffled gloom.
I know I must distance myself from you,
Leaving behind only repercussions and a vague
residue.

In recurring dreams, where normalcy is the
theme,
Can we meet again in the fabric of a dream?
No one will know about our secret meeting
I won't whisper a word about our stolen
greeting.

I hear the muffled melodies we once shared in
song,
My fingers ache for the violin's notes where
they belong.
Now it sits forlorn, buried under dust's heavy
veil,
I could strum the strings till my fingers go pale.

All our dreams lie piled in the dusty expanse,
A distant love now grows faint with every
chance.
As you walk alone on your journey's winding
ride,
Do you picture me beside you, like a shadowed
guide?

Promises once made now fade into the mist,
Our love, a lost ballad that time can't resist.
The pain runs deep, and won't leave for a while,
You live with a stranger now, yet you try to
force a smile.

You mask your longing and you crave my
familiar glance,
But deep down you miss my shadow that
provided you warmth once.

Memory, a merciless mirage

Memory, a merciless mirage,
The sharper the pain, the more it plays its cruel
game.
Attempting to flee, it clings tighter, a relentless
spectre.
Life's fleeting flame and youth's quicksilver
stream,
The ache persists, and memories flood back like
a relentless tide.

When a cherished dish is served, I dream of
sharing it with you,
When our favourite tunes turn, I imagine
singing in tandem.
Passing our beloved pizzeria, I envision you
seated there,
Engaging in conversations with a phantom of
your presence.

Your voice keeps echoing in my ears
You said you were leaving for our own good.
How can we find goodness without one
another?
Perhaps you've found a brighter path,
Perhaps you share pizza with a new partner.
Do you still cherish the same songs in your
playlist?
Or have your melodies changed with your new
muse?
I replay our favourite tunes, grasping at the
ghastly grief.
Do you still greet the sunrise we once adored?
I sleep in, avoiding its golden gaze.
Your voice still echoes in my head and I'm still
ignoring them.

Happy Endings

Shall I steal the moon and bring it near,
Or whisk you to an isle where dreams appear?
Please lift my heart from sorrow's darkened
throng,
And let love's ember in your chest burn strong.

I'll rekindle the flames of our first meeting's
light,
And sing the tunes that turned our nights
bright.
Though mournful melodies bring tears anew,
Those symphonies of old will guide me to you.

The lullabies once sweet that eased my plight,
Now lie in silence through the lonely night.
Oh, queen of hearts, how far you've roamed
away—
I'll cross the seas to bring you back one day.

Reject not my love with cruel disdain,
For fragile is my heart, through joy and pain.
Treat it kindly, not with daggers keen,
But with soft kisses where affection's seen.

Your smile alone can melt my heart of stone,
I long for your embrace, it feels so lone.
Forget our quarrels, remember only bliss,
For love to last, we must choose the sweetest
kiss.

In your presence, have I not opened wide?
Shared every secret, no longer to hide?
Guard our tale with care; let it not fade to
fiction,
For life without you is but a cruel addiction.

May future eyes believe in love's second
beginnings,
And cherish tales of bittersweet, happy
endings.

Hustle Of Waves

Upon the tranquil bay where thoughts begin to
sway,
A pensive gaze meets the placid sea, where
waves gently play.
In solitude's cuddle, I stand with a vacant
glance,
Hoping for a chance where dreams and
memories dance.
The fluttering breeze whispers secrets to the
sky,
Each stone and wave a witness to time passing
by.
Amid the crowd of echoes, my heart feels alone,
Seeking solace in the sea's unspoken tone.
Through the open door of reflection, I find my
way,
To where the sea's serene beauty makes the
world seem gay.
No wiles or smiles can sway this sedating space,

Where each moment of harmony is a cherished
grace.
The hustle of waves precedes the hustle of the
city,
Where blue collides with yellow, we find the
horizon's beauty.
The constant hush blends with the gentle
breeze,
Soothing and healing the troubled mind with
ease.
The distant mast of a ship catches the eye,
Growing smaller and smaller, merging with the
sky.
The vibrant sun performs its last dance,
Melting into the sea in a final, golden trance.
The sky's vast canvas holds a soft, serene face,
In this sea of solitude, I find my place.
With each glance at the waves, my spirit's bore,
The sea's eternal rhythm is the one I adore.

Skipping The Pretences

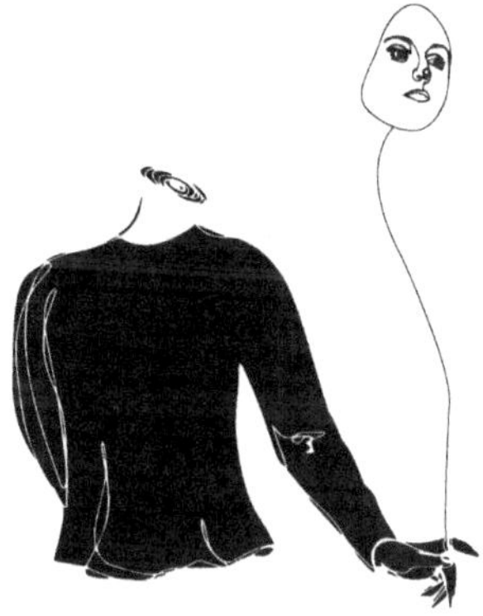

The gentle touches linger in faded, dusty letters,
Or lost in the labyrinth of countless, deleted
chatters.
The pretence has passed, no longer a necessary
art,
You've become a total stranger, a distant,
dispassionate heart.

It's a marvel that we once mused on how we
perfectly paired,
Life chugs on like a train, through stations we
once shared.
The only task is to avoid clinging to any one
stop,
Lest we miss our destination, as we drift and
hop.

We once rhymed sweet verses where "You're my
destination" played,
Yet now, pretence has vanished where affection
once swayed.
No need for late-night calls or love letters long
penned,
The dark chocolates once sweet on your lips
now bitterly offend.

The pretences are discarded, no longer in
demand,
You can stroll past me, and no one will
understand.
As we've journeyed apart, with our once-shared
dreams unspun,
Our past fades into memory, like the setting
sun.

Serenity In Nature's Embrace

Humming our favourite song brings warmth to
the heart,
We cherish the tunes that won't fall apart.
Now the same tune brings a painful tear,
In the serene forest where we once found cheer,
The place feels restless, filled with lonely fear,
Echoes of silence whispering, always near.

The giant banyan, where we carved our names
with pride,
Still recognizes me, offering shade where
memories reside.
Do you ever stop by this banyan while passing
by?
To recall the love we had beneath its sky.

On rainy days, we shared one small shade,
Now the drops fall like bullets, memories fade.
I seek shelter under the weeping tree,
Crying through the night, lost in my plea.

Where shall I go to seek eternal peace,
Is it the snow-capped mountain or the calm,
endless sea?
My heartache echoes with nature's gentle
sound,
Oh Mother Nature, let me rest, in your arms,
profound.

Our Love was A Lost Cause

When we met, our hearts sparked with zeal,
We wove a web of love, a bond that felt real.
Our secret affection, shielded from sarcastic
views,
We cherished it as pure, a divine muse.
Bit by bit, we shared our dreams,
I laid bare my heart, shining with hopes and
beams.
Together we watched movies, shared laughter
and joy,
You completed my thoughts, like a perfect ploy.
In every aspect, we complemented each stride,
Yet life, had its own plans to confide.

Years passed, and our bond grew ever strong,
But misunderstandings, though brief, seemed
to prolong.
As expectations quietly rose, I felt the strain,
Your small fights and frustrations began to
wane.
In your evolving view of love, I found my place
withdrawn,
Slowly, I felt like a misfit, as if love's light was
gone.

I was focused on building my bright career,
Unaware you were drifting, finding solace near.
Days passed, and I struggled to grasp your swift
change,
In letters and messages, I pleaded, feeling
estranged.
You were firm in your need for a pause,
Your words clear: our love was a lost cause.
When silence fell between us, the truth came to
light,
Your love had faded for me, though mine clung
tight.
I had to learn the art of letting go,
Dreams shattered, promises broken, memories
in tow.
Tears dried up, and no comfort came near,
As I wept on my pillow, with hope and fear.

I prayed for your return, but the void remained,
Losing both friend and love left me deeply
pained.
In this relationship, I poured my heart and soul
true,
At last, with heavy hearts, I bid my final adieu.

Relationship Of The Fall

Brick by brick, we built a meaningful
relationship,
Moments of magic drifted by like a gentle
breeze.
Foundations forged in trust and tender
embraces,
A towering tribute to our love's beauty.

Bittersweet burdens breed broken hearts,
And broken hearts bring melancholy and tears.
Your vibrant shadow sways in the dimming
dusk,
While my heart howls quietly, hinting at
hidden fears.

The dream we once cherished is now choked
with weeds.
We planted passion in the rich soil of our souls,
But time and expectations have rendered it
barren.
Where warmth once flourished, now coldness
reigns.
Rivers of affection lie frozen beneath the frost
of lies,
Our relationship resembles the crisp leaves of
fall.

As night deepens, darkness descends,
While your peaceful slumber unfolds,
Mine is filled with tears and restless thoughts.

The Last Dance Of The Echoes

Your voice echoes in my head and I try to
ignore it
As twilight's tender tears tend to twist the
knife of night,
Even a dozen doses of whisky can't dissolve the
ache.
The endless echo of your absence, makes my
body shake,
Though I wail with the wind or plead with the
stars
I lose myself in fast bikes and racing cars.
You won't return; my heart still yearns.
Our once-gloried "us" is a tale that now burns,

Friends and family offer solace, but can't
decode my silent scream
I lack the words to express the pain within.
Nights grow dark, and dreams fade in despair,
Soothing serenades lost in the echoing air.
our melodious murmurs are gone from the
other end of the line.
Frustration fills my heart; I can't find the time.
Why cage my tears and hold back the light?
What joy is there in clinging to the sorrows of
night?

I Love The Idea of You

I wish to flee from your toxic hold,
Yet I'm caught in your love's sweet fold.
A love I chase like a shadow in the mist,
This elusive, drifting dream I can't resist.
It's been days since our dialogue was dear,
Since you shared sweet sentiments, clear.
I sense you drifting, growing far,
Maybe now you've found a new star.

Still, my heart can't fully explain,
It clings to this love like a leech's chain.
Your expectations were a priority and a tether,
While I juggled my life, aiming for better.

With dreams and desires to chase and enhance,
And friends to share stories and dance,
For you, it seemed only "us" mattered,
Though my love was not less, our paths
shattered.

We both loved deeply in our unique ways,
But comprehension eluded through the days.
Perhaps your youth was too narrow to see,
The result was inevitable, as fate's decree.

I still love you, but it's just the thought,
The idea of you, in memory caught.

Garden Of Love

In the garden of my heart where flowers bloom
with grace,
I had given my all, yet you sought a different
place.
If only you had eyes to see, and patience to
understand,
The essence of my love, like petals, is gently
planned.

I waited through the night amidst the cestrum's
sweet, fragrant hall,
Hoping you would come, but you never
answered my call.
In the Titanic of my dreams, our love was
bestirred and proved,
Yet reality revealed lies, and in its shadow, I
moved.

The wait was endless, a small fall from hope to
despair,
I drowned my sorrows in rum, lost in a
labyrinth of care.
Now, I wander through the night, unable to
recognize my way,
In the garden of forgotten love, where I had
once forever hoped to stay.

My Unfinished Wish

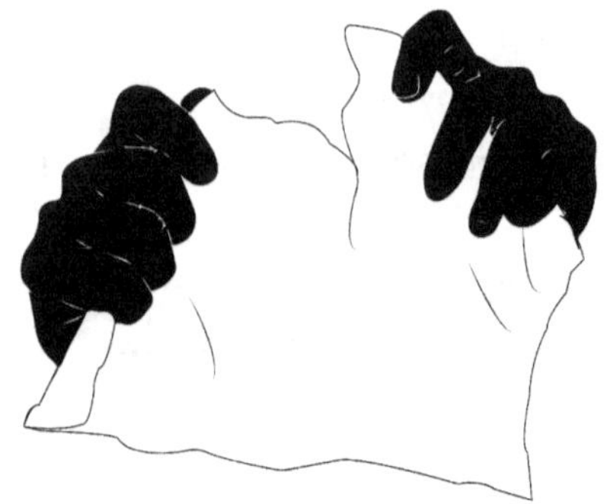

I made my best effort and yet you slipped from
my hands,
While you clasped the careless caress of
someone who didn't even try.
I roamed through forgotten fields of memory,
I made empty promises, painting dreams that
weren't real,
A harsh joke played by the whims of destiny,
Where my heart, once a shining light, drowns
deep in the sea.
I guess I will always keep you as my favourite
unfinished wish,
A shadowed spectre on my soul's shifting
canvas,
A whisper lost in the tumult of time's relentless
roar,
Etched in the fleeting ink of dreams deferred,

A melody half-sung, a love half-lived, a song
unstrung
Whether I will stumble upon love again, I
know not,
Love that came from the depths, you'll never
find again.
Who knows if my heart will beat fast again or if
kisses will return?
Will I stand before the mirror, ready to meet a
love I can't grasp?
Love is a riddle, hard to pin down;
For some, a sweet song; for others, a burning
ache.
True love is a gentle story, pouring grace into
the heart,
Yet it lingers as a longing, knowing it may never
find its home.

Where the heart's sad song mingles with the
breeze,
I'm left with the shadow of a passion, vast and
free.
An eternal love, incomplete and lingering,
A quiet tribute to the endless ache of desire.

Tell Me Not A Lying Tale

Tell me not a lying tale,
A distant love that turned so pale.
I begged the creators to keep you near,
You made my entire universe, my dear.

I still have a story to unveil,
I traded my soul with the devil to no avail.
How hard it could be to love forever,
Yet I did not grasp the effort it would tether.

Maturity was not enough at that age,
Or else I would have turned a wiser page.
I would hold your gift with a grip so tight,
And pray to the heavens to guide us to light.

Could you forgive the sins I have sown,
For promises broken and love not shown?
We wished for eternal joy, forever bright,
Yet life scripts a tale of shadow and light.

Perhaps it's all for a greater good,
Maybe the new me is misunderstood.
Life will reveal a fresh start,
A life without you—can it still hold a part?

Let Me Dream

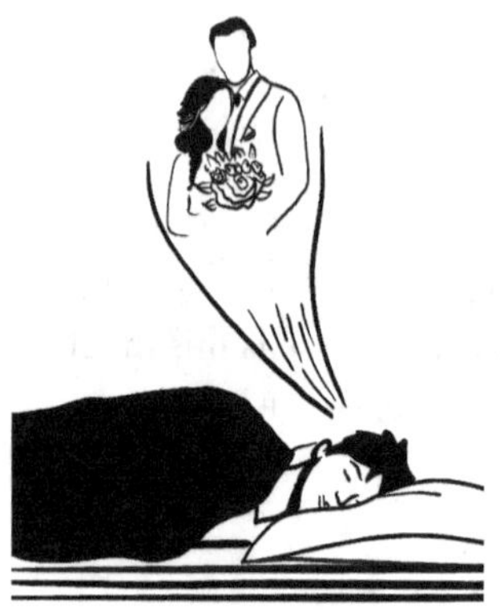

In the spring's advent when the nightingale
sings,
A peacock's plume dances on beauty's fleeting
wings.
Among tuberose blossoms and jasmine's soft
kiss,
Beauty's brief bloom fades, yet love's essence we
miss.

As you stroll by with a rose entwined in your
hair,
Petals murmur secrets of dreams lost in despair.
Love's endless echoes drift through fragrant
fields,
While transient blossoms yield to what true
affection reveals.

In gardens where the bold colours brightly
gleam,
Love's eternal promise outshines the darkest
dream.
Fleeting flames of love flicker in twilight's
tender hue,
Isolation whispers, with a heart broken in two.

Despite the solace found in beer and cigarettes'
embrace,
Pain remains a constant companion, never
erased.
One more drag of smoke seeks to stifle the
ache,
But visions of you linger, leaving my heart to
break.

Nostalgia gnaws through memories, both smiles
and tears,
In intoxicated slumber, I seek solace from fears.
Don't rouse me from dreams where our past
softly gleams,
For dreams cradle me better than harsh, waking
schemes.

Where Butterflies Fly

Take me to the land where butterflies drift in
vibrant silence,
Where caterpillars weave dreams in silk's quiet
brilliance.
In their cocooned haven, they rest in blissful
sorrow,
Waiting to awaken and soar with tomorrow.

Take me to a realm where flowers blush and
greet,
A garden so grand, even Eden feels incomplete.
Where angels softly tread, bestowing gentle
grace,
And deer and fawns frolic in a serene, endless
space.

Where unicorns and centaurs are not mere
shadows,
But living myths in fields where the light always
follows.
Take me to a place where peace is a river
flowing free,
And the fragrance is a potent, timeless plea.
Where melodies rise in a chorus of shared song,
And everyone dances, where judgement is
never wrong.
A heaven where crime and violence are mere
tales from afar,
And equality reigns, a bright, shining star.

Dance In The Rain

When the breeze cools down and clouds hint at
rain,
I yearn to taste the first drops, as they fall like
gentle pain.
Clouds don't conceal their inner storms with
strife,
When they're heavy with sorrow, they release
tears of life.
I'm learning to follow this natural, cleansing
flow,
To let go of my burdens and let my own
sorrows show.
Let's venture out and dance beneath the falling
rain,
Erasing away our fears, and washing off our
pain.
We've forgotten the scent of the blossoms we
once knew,
Daisies and daffodils now seem like stranger's
view.

The earthy aroma of rain-kissed summer's end,
Soothes our senses and hearts, making broken
souls mend.
Pause a moment longer, breathe deep, and
listen close,
To the robin and the sparrow, as their melodies
transpose.
Who knows, if we listen deeply, their songs may
impart,
That creatures too have wisdom, and not just
the human heart.
So let's dance in the rain, leave past shadows
behind,
Why cling to yesterdays when new joys we can
find?
Let's strive to make a poor soul's heart lift with
a smile,
Knowing in the end, our lives and efforts are
worthwhile.
As we journey to the dust, let's go with a
generous heart,
Bringing joy and light to others, playing our
part.
For in this grand dance of life, each soul we
uplift,
Adds to the beauty of existence, a precious gift.

Chronological Cacophony

After endless days of aching pain,
And countless doses numbing the strain,
After rehab's solace and the thought to pursue,
We convince ourselves we've grown, matured
too.

Yet as time marches on with its unyielding
grace,
We drift with the tide, in life's endless race.
Years later, staring at your mirrored face,
Will you reflect on the paths we didn't
embrace?

The promises made, now shadows in the past,
For you, new independence came at last.
I wonder where that choice has led your way,
To a brighter future, where love holds sway.

If fate should bring our paths to cross once
more,
Will memories' weight rise from deep,
forgotten before?
Will your heart ache if our eyes meet and lock,
Or feel pangs of envy if I've found a new rock?

Will you regret the choice that left you alone,
Wishing for a love you once called your own?

The Last Dance

One last time, I wish to see your face,
To return your memories with gentle grace.
I'll place your hands upon my heart, so near,
And let you listen to its rhythm clear.

One last time, let's dance to our favourite song,
Where melodies of old and sweet memories
belong.
I'll gaze into your eyes, seeking a final truth,
And say goodbye to the play of feelings and
youth.

No longer will you decide our shared fate,
I won't let your choices shape love's slate.
Though I love you now and may love you still,
Time may dim love, but I wish you peace until.

If in future years, our paths cross anew,
It won't change the wish I have for you.
In the end, your happiness is all I seek,
For our love's end has made me strong, not
weak.

Lost In Oblivion

They say I once loved a lady and we were set to
wed,
But I can't recall a thing, lost in oblivion's
thread.
I wander through the dusty halls of this
forsaken place,
Making fleeting friends, as their faces lose trace.

My mouth is filled with bitter pills,
Always drowsy under these hospital thrills.
I heed the nurses' orders and play in the
garden's green,
While visitors come and go, a lady in particular,
serene.

She brings me old letters, of a love once bright
and fair,
I savour the scent of pages, and the
handwriting's tender care.
Yet, the girl I once adored remains a shadow in
my mind,
Was our love a timeless wonder, or merely left
behind?

Her tears speak volumes, though my memory is
bereft,
I try to comfort her, though my past is left
unkept.
She kisses my forehead gently, then bids me
adieu,
Her visit follows the next week, with the same
letters to view.

An elderly woman now, her hair a cloak of grey,
My own locks are white as snow, and wrinkles
to display.
I know not who this lady is, and she reveals no
name,
Yet her caring presence tells me, her affection
remain.

They say I once loved a lady and we were set to
marry,
But I can't recall a thing, lost in oblivion's quarry.

Amnesia Is A Bliss

People say amnesia is a terrible disease,
Yet, for some, it can bring a rare kind of ease.
Sometimes to forget is a blissful release,
For memory can be both a gift and a curse, with
no peace.

The more we strive to erase, the more it stays,
Imprinted deep in our minds, a tangled maze.
The greatest challenge lies in a tempting past,
Where faces linger and memories hold fast.
No matter how I try to wash them away,
In the corners of my mind, they gently sway.

A face I used to see, think, and dream of so
near,
Now that it's forgotten, I'm unsure how to steer.
Should I feel joy or sorrow, in this emotional
fray?
This is the essence of love in its most painful
display.

As the loving face fades, day by day,
And nothing can halt this inevitable decay.
I can't revisit the images, for I made them burn,
Nor meet the person, as she will never return.

Memories ebb and flow like the tide's gentle
sweep,
Some pinch a little, others cut deep.
Yet, surprisingly, some leave a smile in their
wake,
Often, I find myself laughing, though unsure of
the stake.

Is it laughter of joy or hidden tears that weave?
I can't tell apart the emotions that deceive.
Amnesia's a knife, both cruel and refined,
It brings forth new dawns or nightmares
entwined.

You Stay Alive In My Memory Forever

If I am not there anymore, you stay alive in my
memory forever.
The warmth of your embrace, the gentle caress
of your lips,
In my open arms, you found solace and peace.
Now I drift in the breeze, a whisper in the
cosmos, longing to reach you.
If you wish to halt my journey and hold me
close, please do.
If you close your eyes and my face appears
Understand that I lingered just to say hello.

In my solitude, I struggled to share my thoughts
with kin,
Couldn't articulate this ache, nor let it go.
Only clinging to the bittersweet echoes of our
time.
And if a kind heart dares to inquire your name,
I smile,
A smile that carries the weight of unshed tears.
I utter your beloved, haunting name again,
Memories flash like fleeting stars,
And in that moment, I choose to release it all.
If I am not there anymore, you stay alive in my
memory, forever.

Reality Check

My imagination soared high up in the sky,
Yet dreams dimmed down as reality passed by.
Life, a strict teacher, with lessons harsh and dry,
Now flying in the sky feels like a distant lie,
As life's harsh truths land like a blow,
We search for meaning in life's turbulent flow.
The questions about true love you pose are too
rhetorical,
And I start to laugh—my new disguise for
emotions, almost farcical.
Do you truly want answers to those queries so
profound?
I've learned to butter things up, even for my
own sound.
Life's just a reality check; sweet dreams
sometimes hypnotic,
Yet moments of clarity can feel so iconic.
Now I only watch fantasy films with happy,
bright endings,

Lost in daytime reveries, until someone's wake
brings me to mendings.
I'd rather not be woken up from this sweet,
slumbered grace,
For it's the only time a smile graces my face.
Is it so wrong to daydream, to escape into a
fantasy realm?
Is it forbidden to seek solace, to let imagination
helm?
I adore tales of time travel, wishing I could
rewind,
But then, I'd miss the growth, and the lessons
intertwined.
I'd repeat my mistakes, choose play over
studytime,
Fall for the same love, stumble, and lose my
prime.
Is growing up truly crucial, must we maturely
behave?
Life seems to demand this path, but why is
childhood so brave?
Kindergarten kids, the happiest souls we see,
They dance in pure joy, as carefree as they can
be.
My imagination once soared high in the sky,
I wish to remain there, where dreams gently lie.

Playing Life's Game

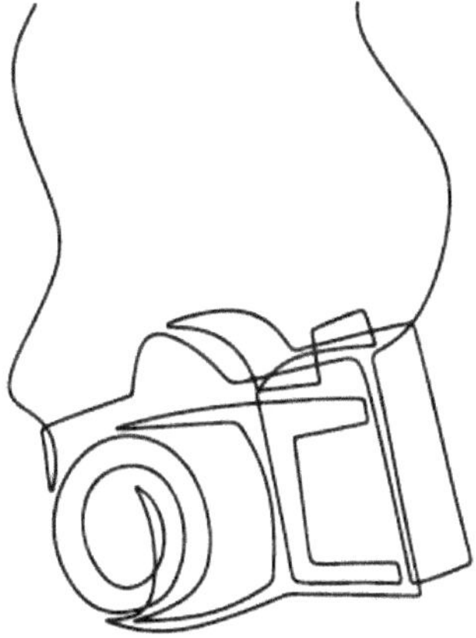

I choose to run from cyanide, embracing life
instead,
For some days feel like slow poison, a heavy
dread.
No elixir is offered, so poison's what we
embrace,
I'll take my chances, with a daring face,
Playing life's game, like Russian roulette in its
place.
I'll let guitar chords strum as I dance along the
beat,
One day at a time, fighting battles sweet.
Transforming into this new version of me,
In life's grand theatre, where we all must see.

So what if the plot shifts or a new drama is
cast?
We'll play our roles, as the audience's gaze is
vast,
We keep performing and acting gradually,
Wearing our masks in a world changing
radically.
Some days we wear makeup; some days we
don't,
Some days are filled with drugs, others we
won't.
Stars keep twinkling as we lose ourselves in the
night,
Then reality rolls back, and we face life's fight.
Through every scene, no matter the strife,
We keep playing, ever faithful, in the theatre of
life.

I Dare To Explore

To the carnival of chaos, where creatures cavort
and cry,
We danced in delirium, each role a fleeting fly.
One day we'll part ways, no longer in the show,
We crossed the crossroads, where varied winds
did blow.

Dreams and desires danced in the dim, dark air,
We built a bridge to balance, where pathways
weren't fair.
Chose the lesser-trodden trail, where few dared
to stray,
It made a marked difference in my journey
today.

Now I stride, stalwart and strong, my visage a
vibrant light,
God's love lifts me, in the day and the night.

Do you envy the glow, or wish for my fall?
Did you desire my defeat, a crumpled, cringing
thrall?
Shoulders slumping, tears tumbling, sorrow's
silent stream?
Weakened by wailing whispers, crushed
beneath a dream.

Forgive the frown of your frustration, I rise,
rekindle and glow,
I trust in life's journey; hope you go with the
flow,
Life's more grand, in this labyrinth of lore,
I embrace the risks, and I'm glad I did explore.

Lost In Your Charm

When I gaze at your face, I'm spellbound in
awe,
All reason and logic crumble, caught in your
draw.
Whatever promises I made to myself, so
steadfast and true,
Crumble like sandcastles when I catch sight of
you.
My head turns like a magnet when you enter
the room,
My eyes stay glued to you, chasing away all
gloom.
People might call me a stalker, tracing your
trail,
But my eyes stay anchored, in your presence,
they sail.
I cannot take my eyes off you, lost in your
enchanting allure,
Though I rehearse the finest lines, my resolve
feels unsure.

In a moment of weakness, your enchantment
takes hold,
My heart surrenders to you, as your charm
unfolds.
Your fragrance lifts a smile, a scent so divine,
The lavender notes are nostalgic, a memory's
sign.
When you speak with clarity, I falter, words
entwined,
What is this power that leaves my confident
self behind?
When you place your hand on my shoulder,
casual and light,
My body melts like ice in a furnace, weak in its
plight.
I don't know if you'll ever be mine, this I can't
foresee,
But I wish for your face to always smile with
glee.
I long to be lost in your serene embrace,
And each time I see you, I find my place.
Spellbound by your essence, in a wondrous
enchantment,
I lose myself in whispers, caught in your
advancement.

Until I Met You

Until I met you, the pictures were all black and
white,
Until I met you, tears rolled till midnight,
Until I met you, I never realised that love can
happen like this,
Until I met you love was never an eternal bliss.

With past romantic encounters, I wore a
blindfold,
Previously, my dignity and self-belief I sold,
I tried to restrain the bond like holding sand in
my palm,
Until I met you, I could not keep my calm.

Until I met you, I knew not of friendship
within love,
Until I met you I had fear and anxiety above,
Until I met you, love songs only had a sorrow
tune,
Until I met you my heart sank in the sands of
dune.

Since I met you, my life has been newly
molded,
I have embraced life and not kept my arms
folded.

As I have met you, I listen to happier songs
now,
I believe destiny has brought us together
somehow,
I now believe in the morning sun and the
shining night moon,
Now that I have met you, I can't wait to see you
soon.

Letters To My Grave

When I donned the soldier's vest, your joy did
light the skies,
To friends, I spun your tales with fondness in
my eyes.
Monthly letters rained between us, brimming
with delight,
And each awaited word from you turned my
dull days to light.

Upon my leave, you'd greet me with a warm hug
so tight,
We'd watch the sea together, beneath the
lighthouse shining bright.
Waves would kiss our feet, your hand would
trace our names in sand,
A fleeting, splendid moment, carved by love's
gentle hand.

In my final relentless task, I failed to pen a line,
When I returned from battle's storm, your
smile I couldn't find.
I came to find your home abandoned, empty
and bare,
I sought your friends for answers, but your
presence was not there.

A bitter truth was told: you've wed a man from
the countryside,
How could you break a bond so deep, and cast
our love aside?
Was it wealth that lured you, or your kin's
unyielding plea?
After years of heartfelt vows, you turned your
back on me.

Now by the sea, I linger, life is a ship that's lost
its course,
Your visage haunts my teary eyes with a silent,
mournful force.
In solitude I dwell, where land and sky are grim
and cold,
No hunger grips my weary soul, nor dreams
that dare unfold.

Even bullet scars cannot wound as deeply as
this ache,
Why pledge your heart if promises are quick to
break?
My cries are swallowed by the sea, lost in its
endless wave,
Regret fills my every breath; I wish the war had
been my grave.

Let's Give Life A New Meaning

We spend days in the paradox of escapism,
This self-centred act is excessively egocentric.
There are thousands enduring endless agony,
Some skip meals for days, while others crave
parental affection.
Some seek justice amidst gross injustice,
But the corrupt world slams its gates shut on
their pleas.

Rise and start living for their sake,
We will uncover new meanings in the
playground of life.
Life is not merely about personal triumphs or
hollow victories.
Let's begin to dream dreams for others and aid
in their achievements.

When pain and sorrow are constant
companions,
And our days are numbered in the ledger of
time,
Why dwell on past regrets or unfulfilled love?
There is a boundless abundance of affection
surrounding us.

Let's grasp it and discover our joy in others'
happiness,
Giving life meaning in its fleeting, fragile form.